Scope and Sequence

Level 2

UNIT	SOUND(S)	DECODABLE WORDS	OTHER WORDS	SIGHT WORDS
Hello	a b c d e f g h i j k l m n o p q r s t u v w x y z	dog, man, can, mom, pan, map, rod, cap, red, pen, nut, bus, ten, sad, wax, wag, win, web, fox, vet, mix, six, jug, fan, hen, rug, log, bat	apple, ant, arrow, bus, ball, bed, cat, cap, cup, dog, doll, door, elephant, egg, elbow, foot, fish, five, goat, gate, girl, hat, hand, hoop, insect, igloo, ink, juice, jump, jacket, kite, key, king, leg, lion, light, mouth, milk, mouse, nose, nut, nest, octopus, ox, olive, pencil, pizza, panda, quilt, queen, question, rabbit, rice, robot, sun, soap, seed, table, tomato, tiger, umbrella, up, underwear, van, violin, vest, wheel, window, water, fox, box, six, yogurt, yoyo, yellow, zoo, zebra, zipper	
Unit 1	*c, k, ck*	cat, cup, sock, neck, cot, kid, duck, kick, rock, back, lick fig, rat, bed	kite, key	the, is, on, it's, a, can
Unit 2	*sw, st, sk, sp*	swim, stop, skip, spin, stack Pip, Jack, Lin	swing, star, skunk, spider	can, on, her, what, you, do
Unit 3	*tr, fr, dr, cr*	truck, frog, drum, dress, crab, track, drop, drip pond, hop, skip	train, friends, crayon, crawl, fruit	in, the, on, I
Unit 4	*sl, bl, fl, cl*	sled, black, flag, clock, slug, flap, clap, slip, block, cluck red, hen, pot, wind, tick-tock	slide, blue, flower, cloud, fly	the, is, on, in
Unit 5	*sh*	brush, trash, shopping, shed, dish, fish, shell, ship, flash, shelf, crash, smash sun, dog, eggs, bad	shoe, sheep, shark, starfish	is, this, my, on, the
Unit 6	*ch*	ostrich, branch, chin, chest, bench, check, lunch, chick shop, robin, red, six, nest, bugs, get, big	children, cheese, chair, torch	the, has, a, she, in, her, have, for
Unit 7	*th* (unvoiced)	bath, moth, math, think, cloth, path, thick, thin sick, shelf, sink	three, think, thorn, teeth chair, hair	a, on, the, in, my, I
Unit 8	*th* (voiced)	this, that, with den, thin, man, hat, thinks, sun, hot, big, wet, splash, sad, get, bus	clothes, mother, father, feather, these, the, Heather, brothers, they, weather	the, is, these, are, her, they, she
Unit 9	*ng*	ring, king, hang, bang, strong, gong, long, wing, sing, along, song, thing with, hop, skip, run, track, kick, swim, back, drum, lots, fun, but, best		it, me, yes, I, and, on, the, a, my, of, is

Hello

1 1.01 Listen and point. 2 Listen and repeat. Trace.

Aa

3 Trace, write, and say.

A

a

4 1.02 Listen and point. 5 Listen and repeat. Trace.

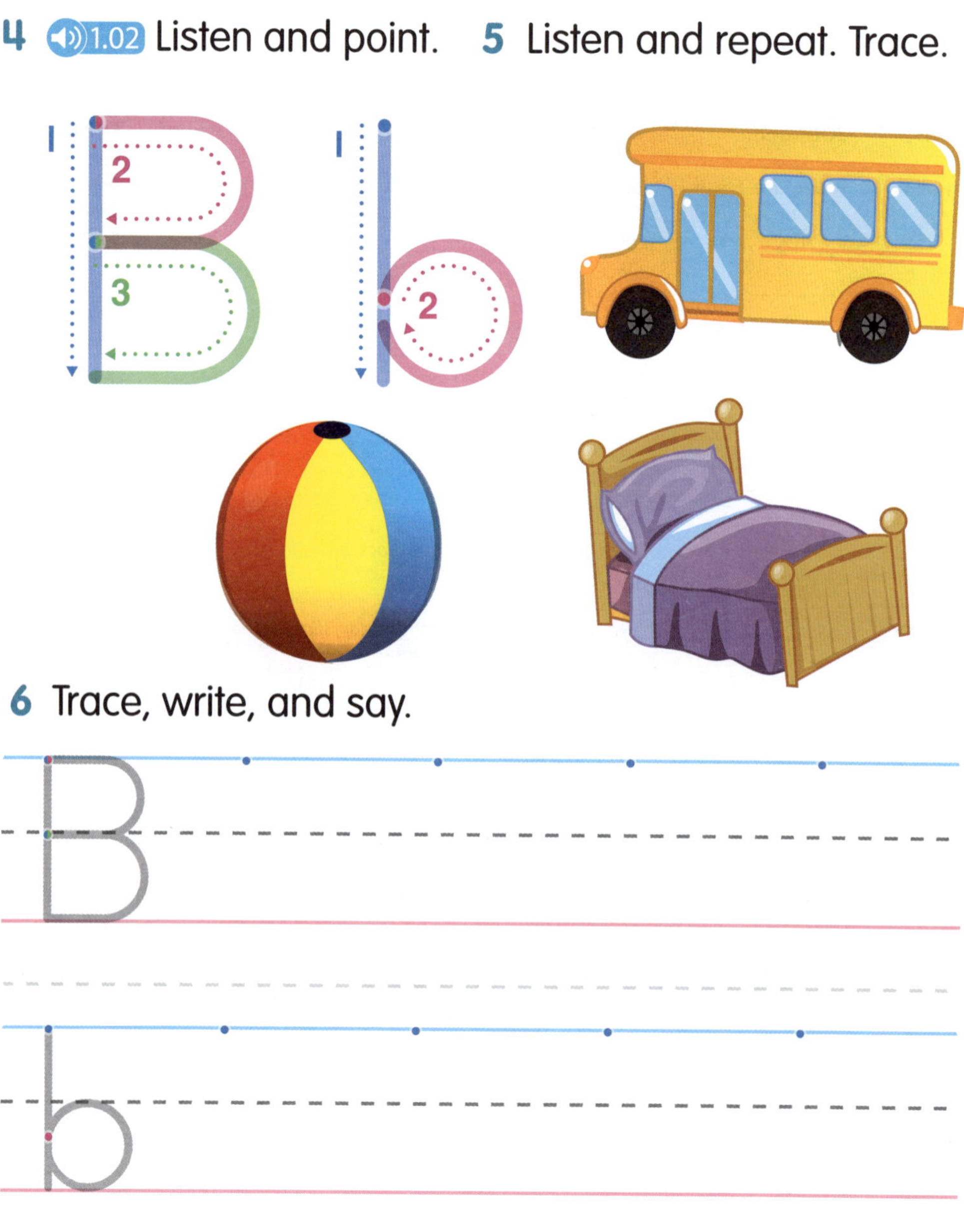

6 Trace, write, and say.

B

b

Vocabulary: apple, ant, arrow, bus, ball, bed

1 1.03 Listen and point. 2 Listen and repeat. Trace.

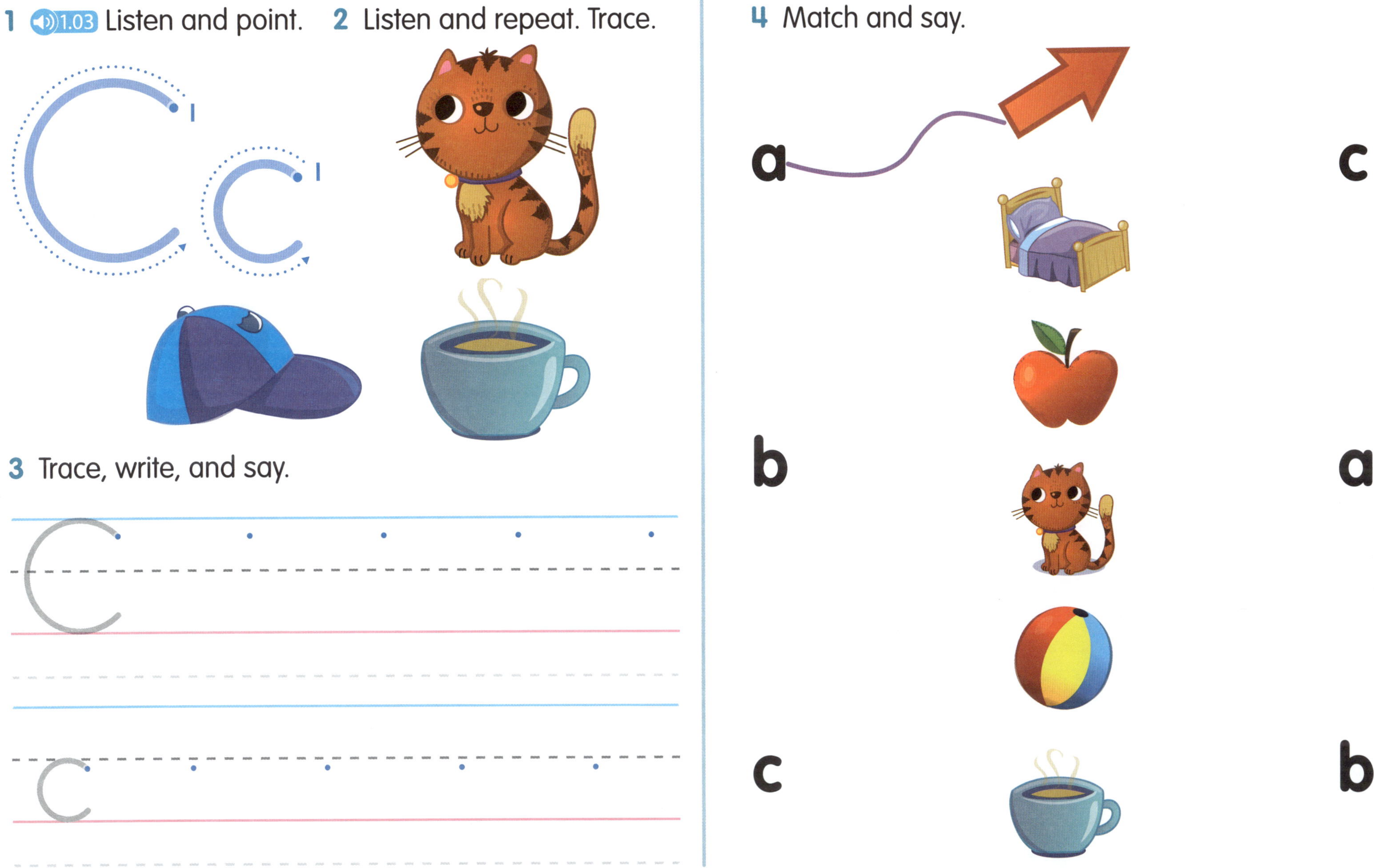

3 Trace, write, and say.

4 Match and say.

1 1.04 Listen and point. 2 Listen and repeat. Trace.

4 1.05 Listen and point. 5 Listen and repeat. Trace.

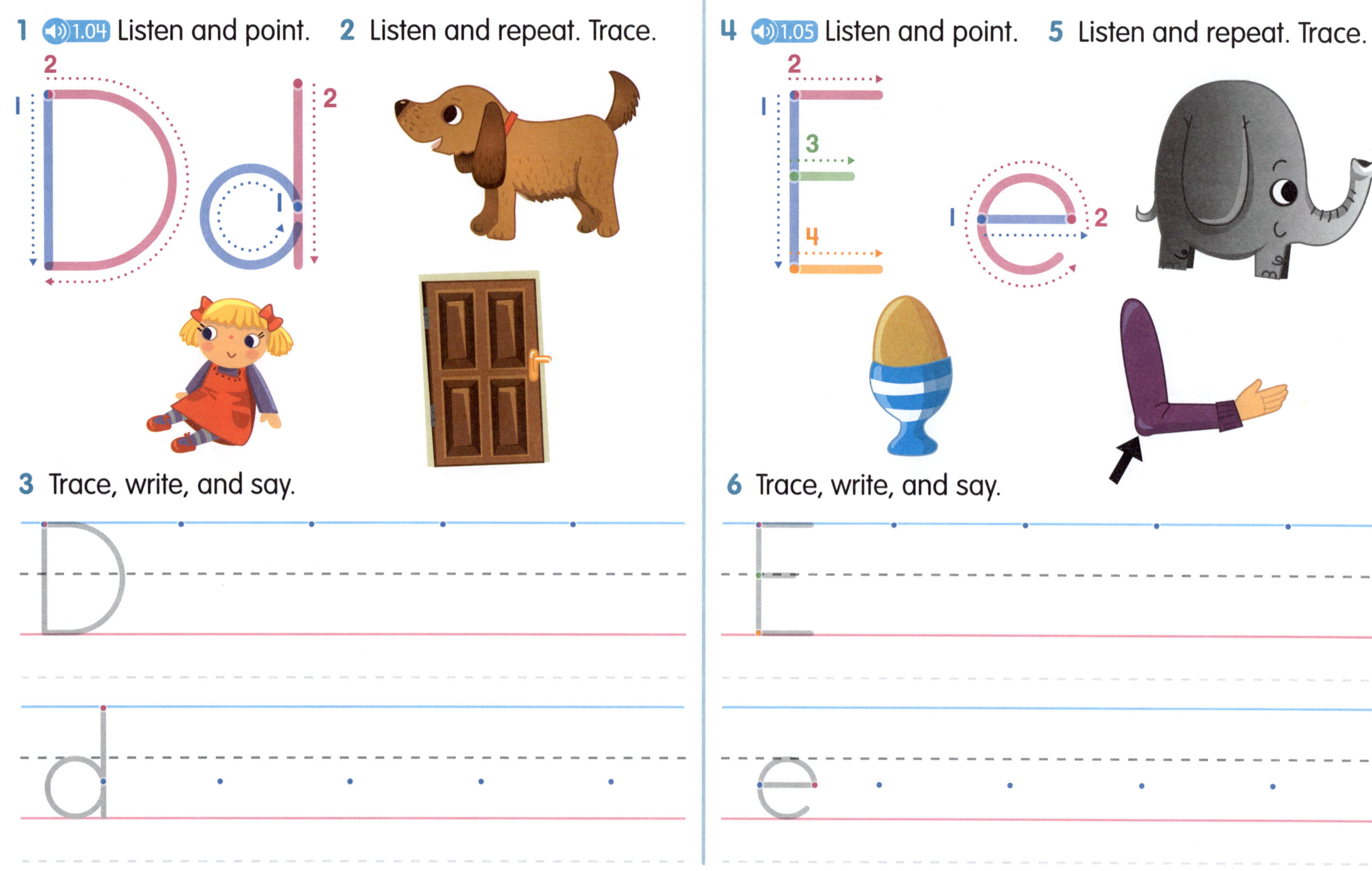

3 Trace, write, and say.

6 Trace, write, and say.

Vocabulary: dog, doll, door, elephant, egg, elbow

1 1.06 Listen and point. 2 Listen and repeat. Trace.

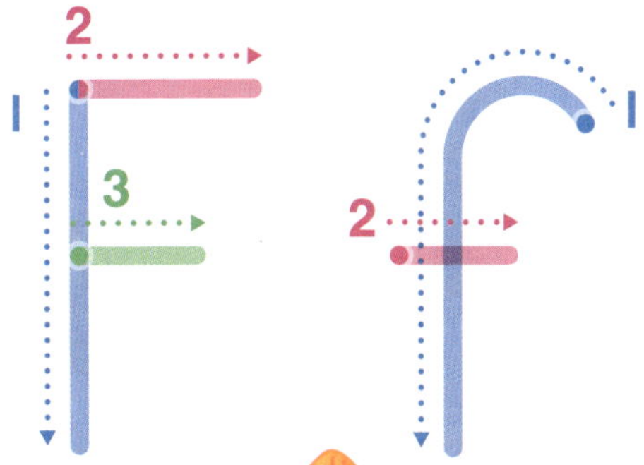

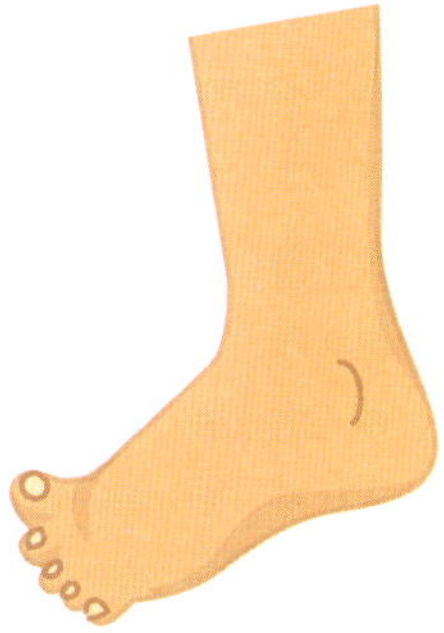

F f

3 Trace, write, and say.

F

f

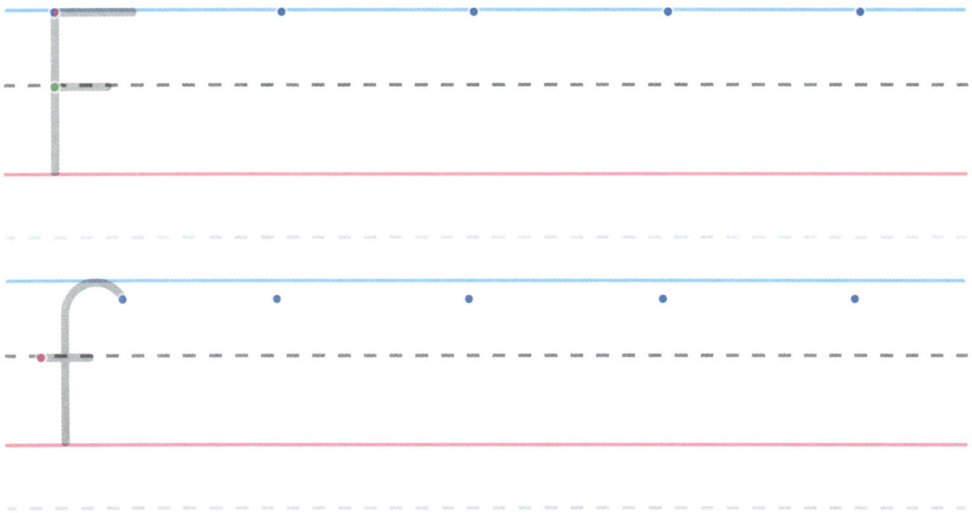

4 1.07 Listen and trace the correct letter.

1 
e c

2 
b d

3 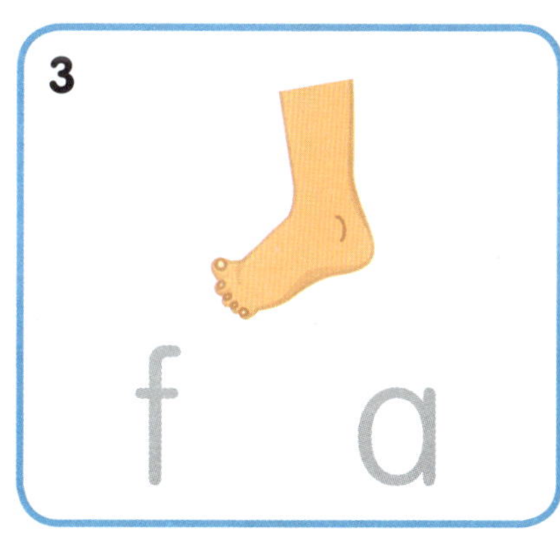
f a

4 
e f

5 
b e

6 
d c

Vocabulary: **foot, fish, five,** elephant, egg, doll, dog

1 1.08 Listen and point. 2 Listen and repeat. Trace.

4 1.09 Listen and point. 5 Listen and repeat. Trace.

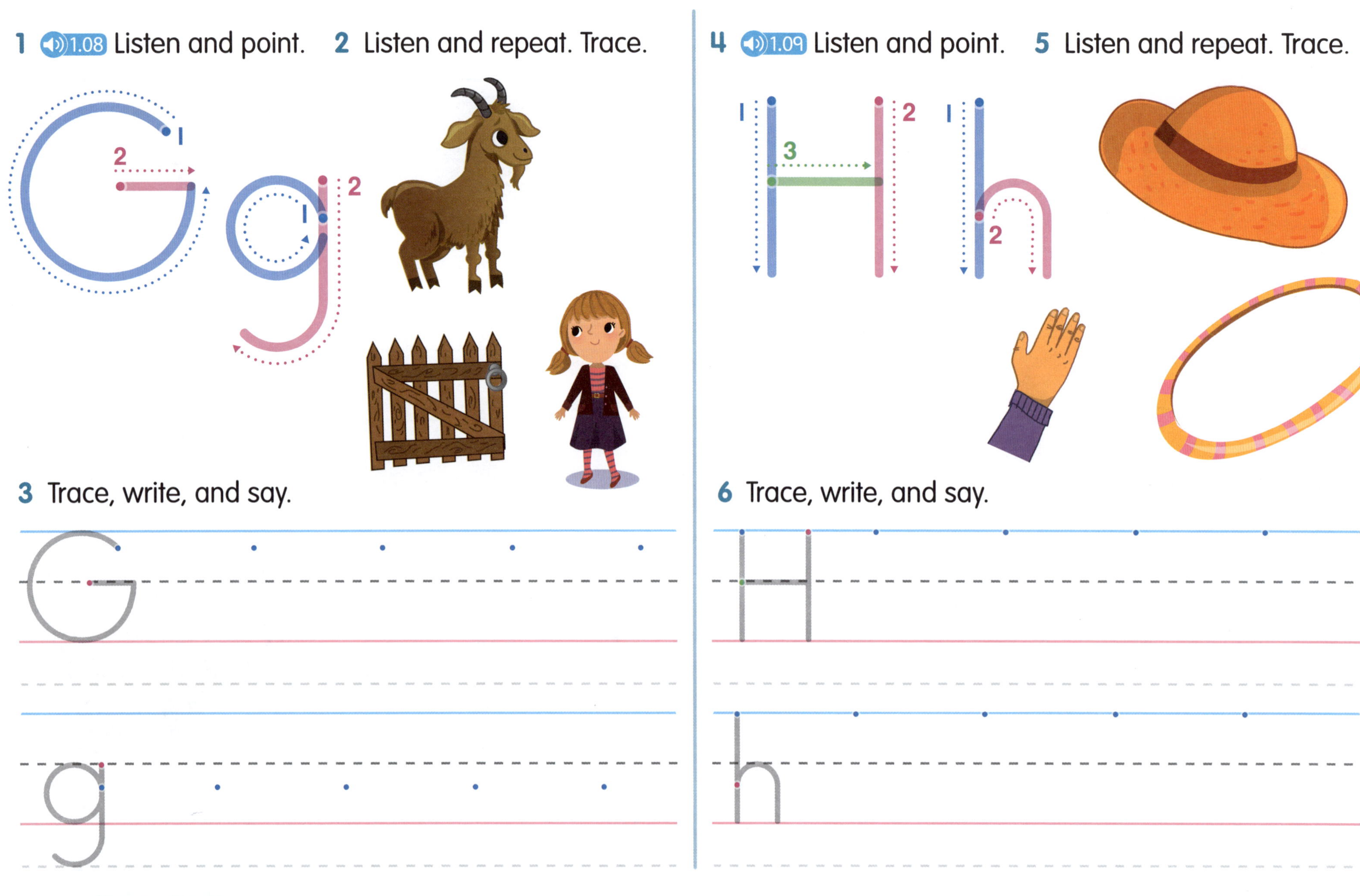

3 Trace, write, and say.

6 Trace, write, and say.

Vocabulary: goat, gate, girl, hat, hand, hoop

1 1.10 Listen and point. 2 Listen and repeat. Trace.

3 Trace, write, and say.

4 Circle the correct picture.

Vocabulary: **insect, igloo, ink,** elephant, goat, doll, apple, ball, hat, girl, cat

1 1.11 Listen and point. 2 Listen and repeat. Trace.

4 1.12 Listen and point. 5 Listen and repeat. Trace.

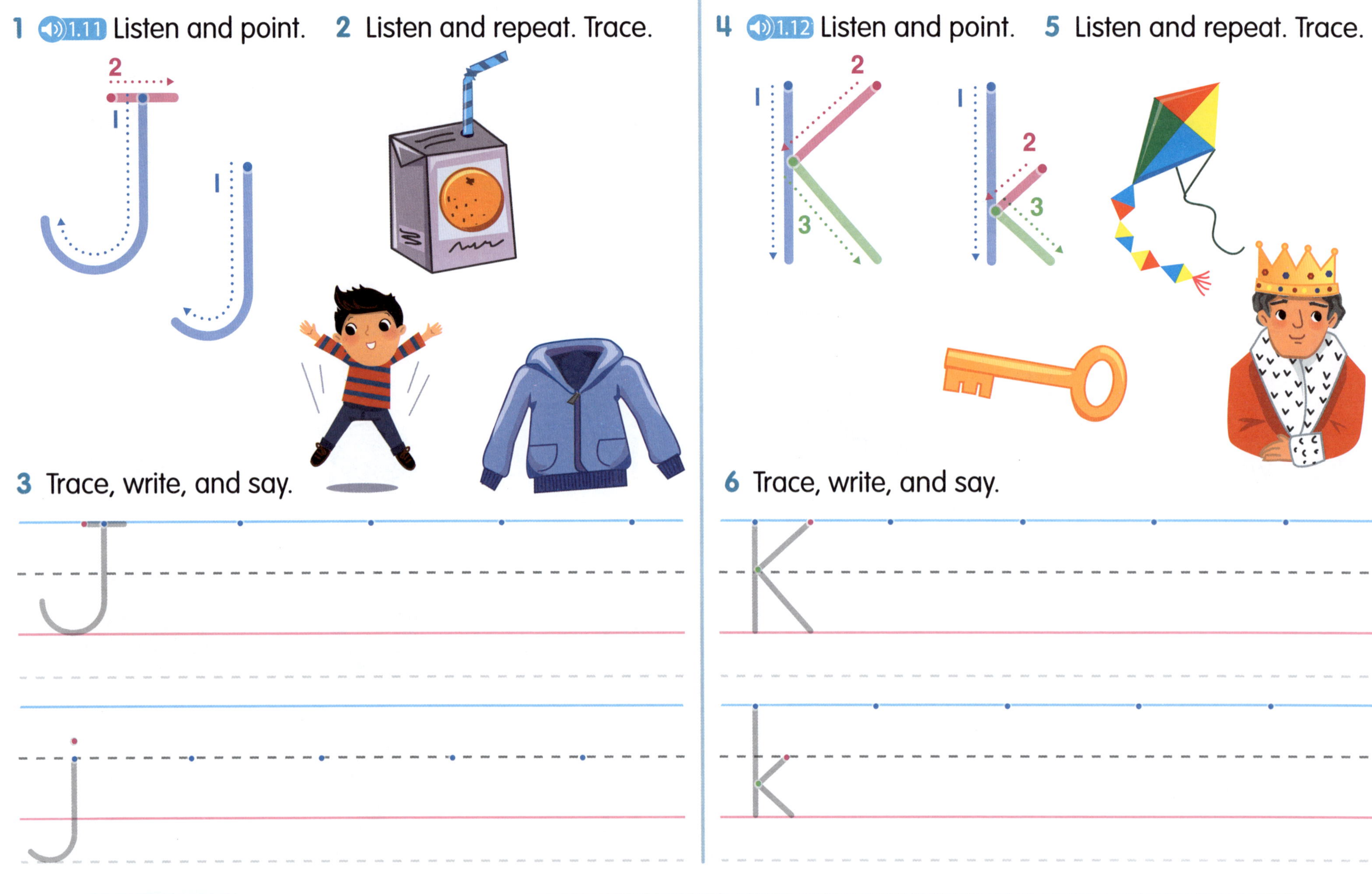

3 Trace, write, and say.

6 Trace, write, and say.

Vocabulary: juice, jump, jacket, kite, key, king

1 1.13 Listen and point. 2 Listen and repeat. Trace.

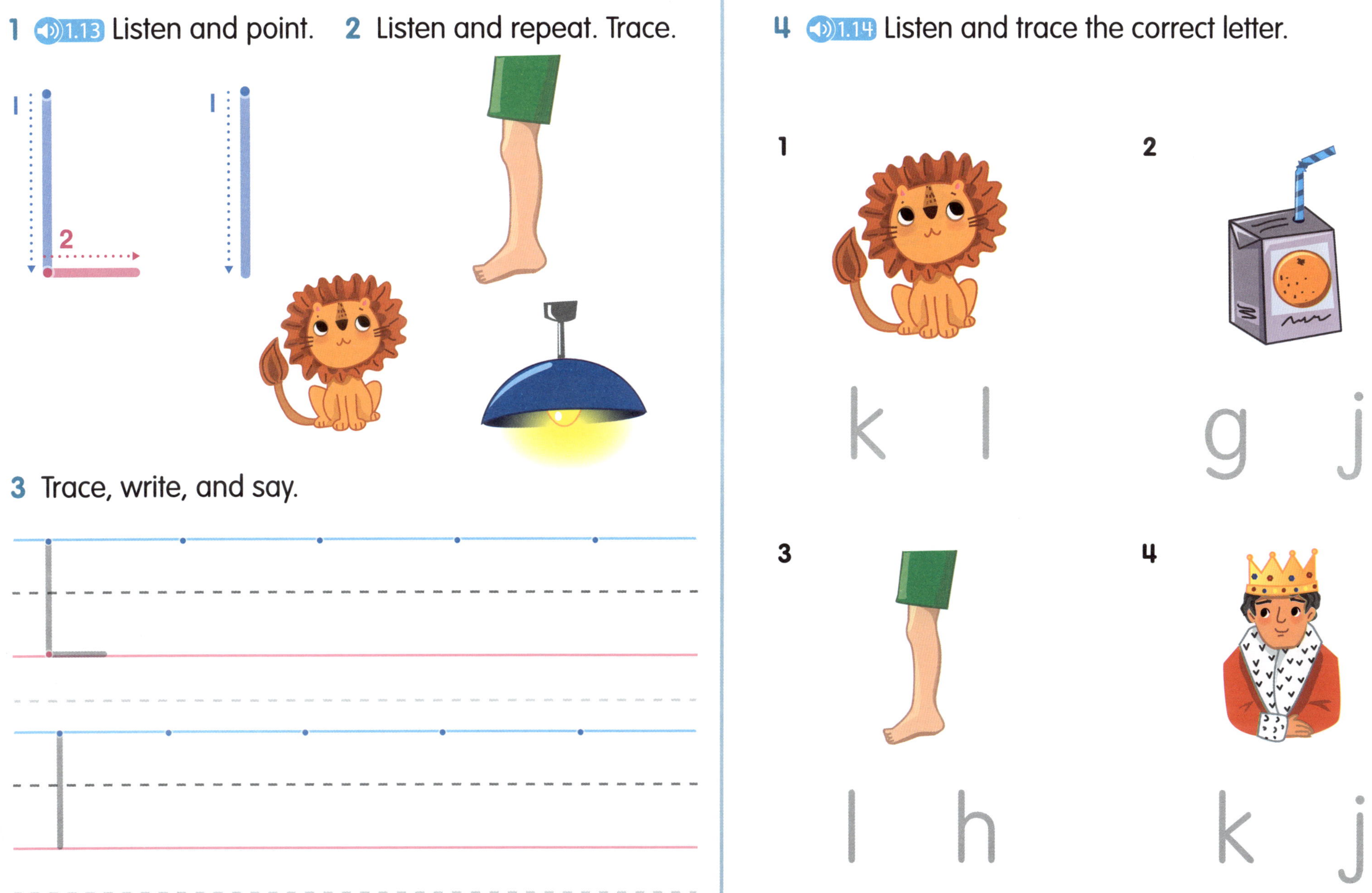

3 Trace, write, and say.

4 1.14 Listen and trace the correct letter.

1 2 3 4

1 1.15 Listen and point.

2 Listen and repeat. Trace.

4 1.16 Listen and point.

5 Listen and repeat. Trace.

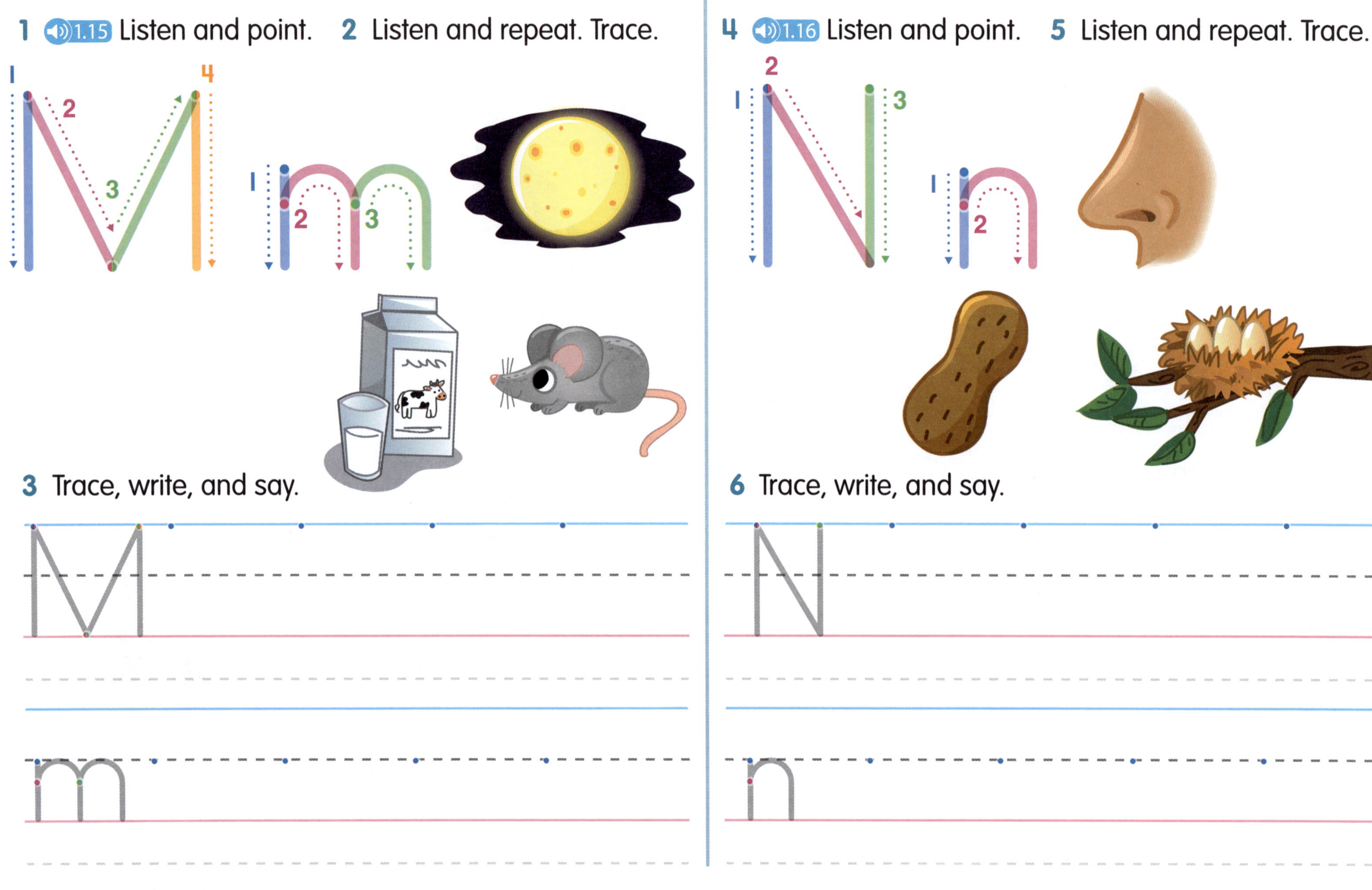

3 Trace, write, and say.

6 Trace, write, and say.

Vocabulary: moon, milk, mouse, nose, nut, nest

1 🔊1.17 Listen and point. 2 Listen and repeat. Trace.

O o

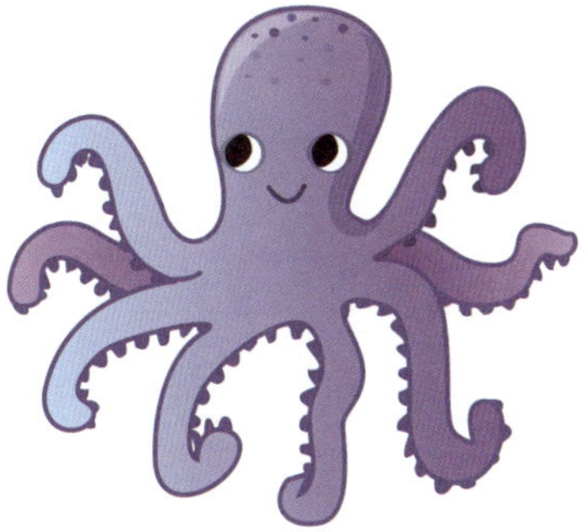

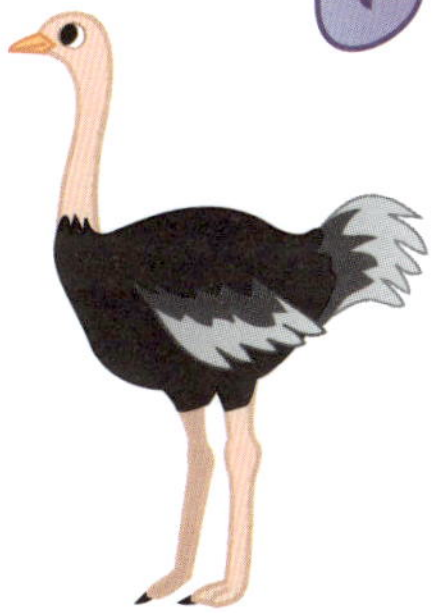

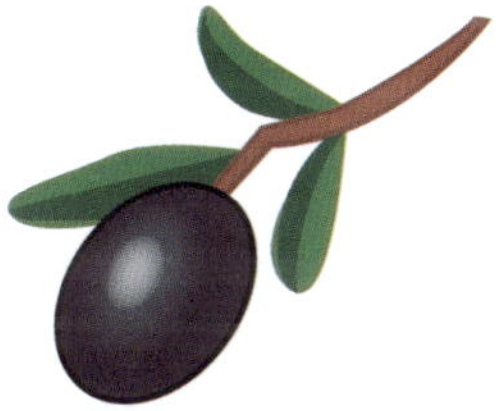

3 Trace, write, and say.

O

o

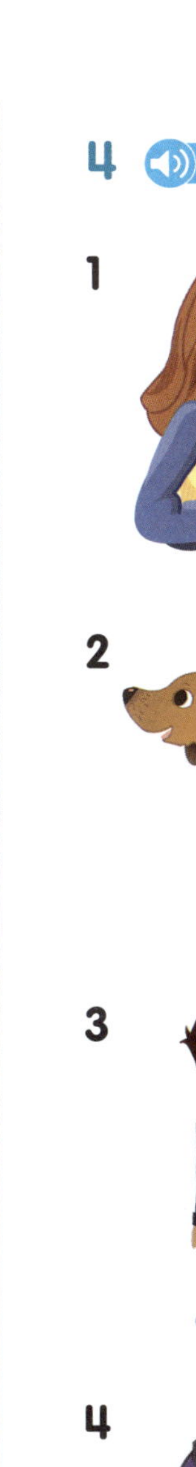

4 🔊1.18 Listen, read, and match.

1	•	• dog
2	•	• mom
3	•	• can
4	•	• man

Vocabulary: octopus, ostrich, olive, mom, dog, man, can

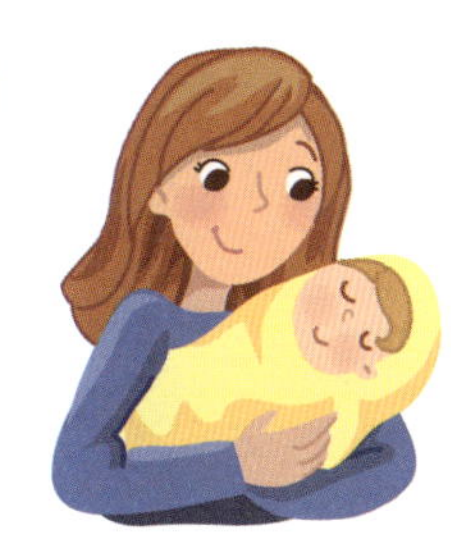

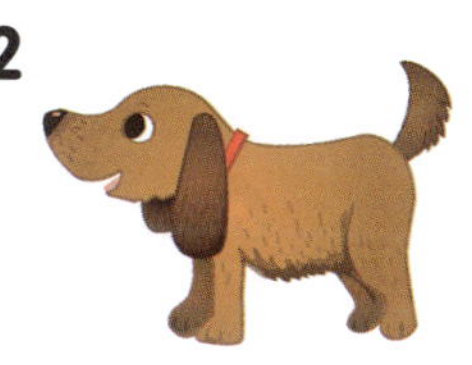

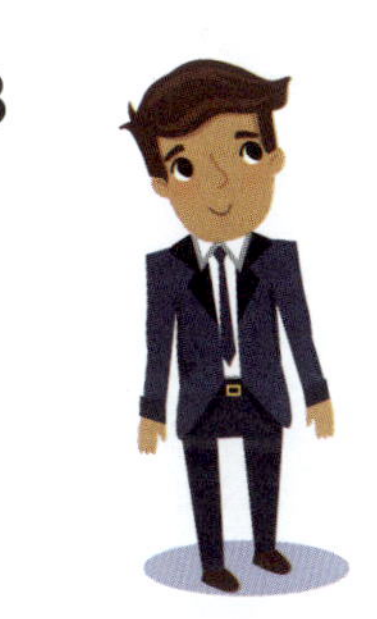

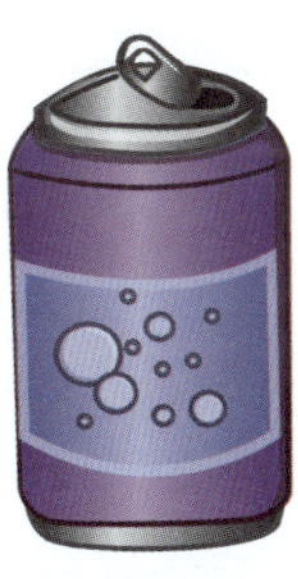

1 1.19 Listen and point. 2 Listen and repeat. Trace.

4 1.20 Listen and point. 5 Listen and repeat. Trace.

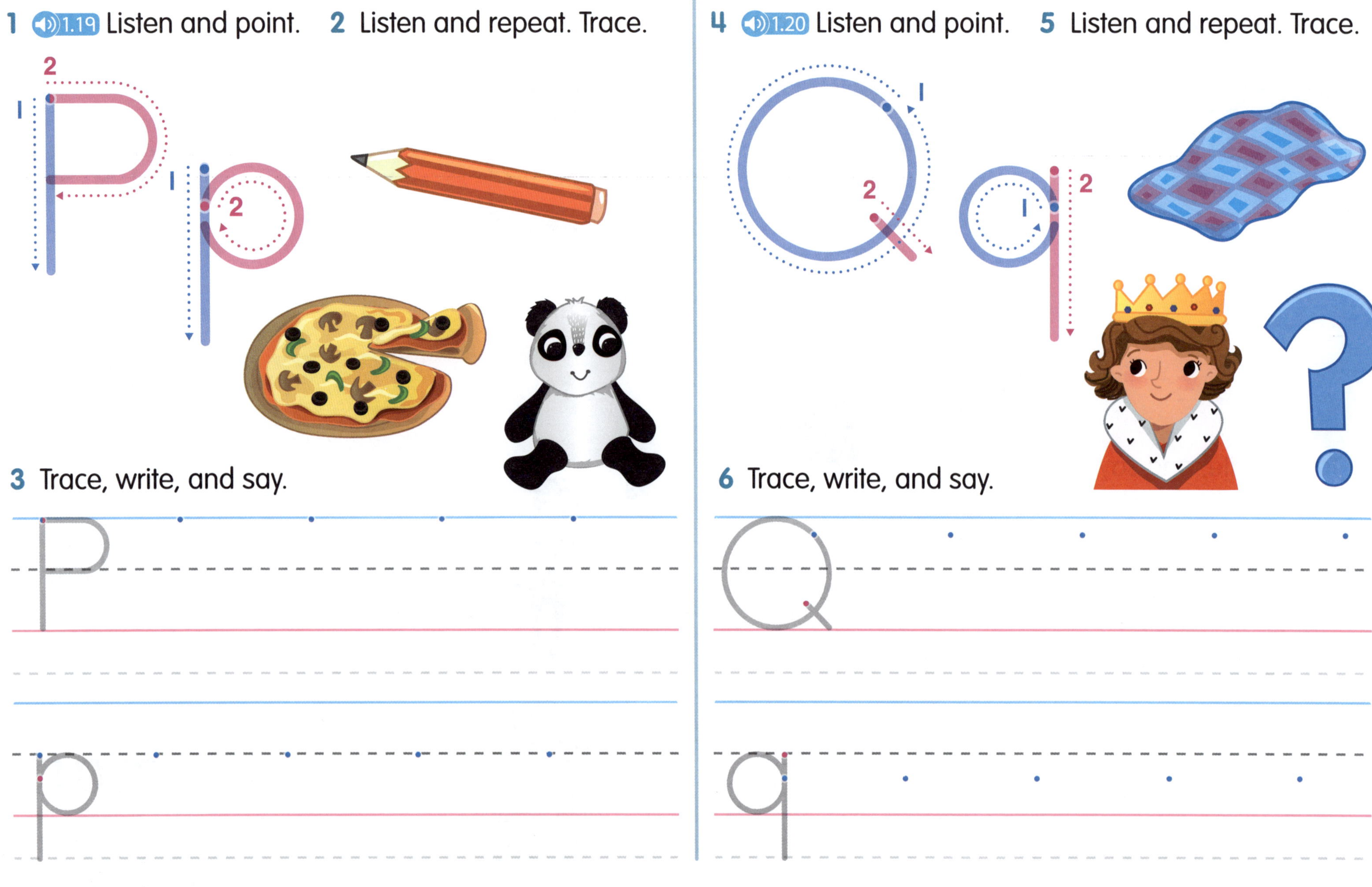

3 Trace, write, and say.

6 Trace, write, and say.

Vocabulary: pencil, pizza, panda, quilt, queen, question

1 1.21 Listen and point. 2 Listen and repeat. Trace.

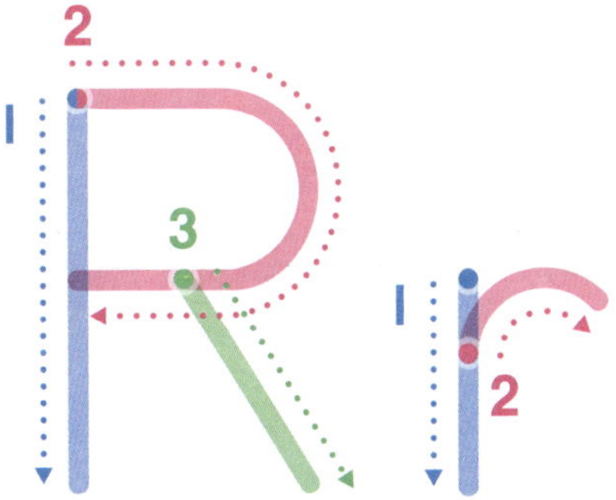

R r

3 Trace, write, and say.

R

r

4 1.22 Listen, read, and circle.

1 

pan

2 

dog rod

3 

pan cap

4 

red pen

1 1.23 Listen and point. 2 Listen and repeat. Trace.

S s

3 Trace, write, and say.

S

s

4 1.24 Listen and point. 5 Listen and repeat. Trace.

T t

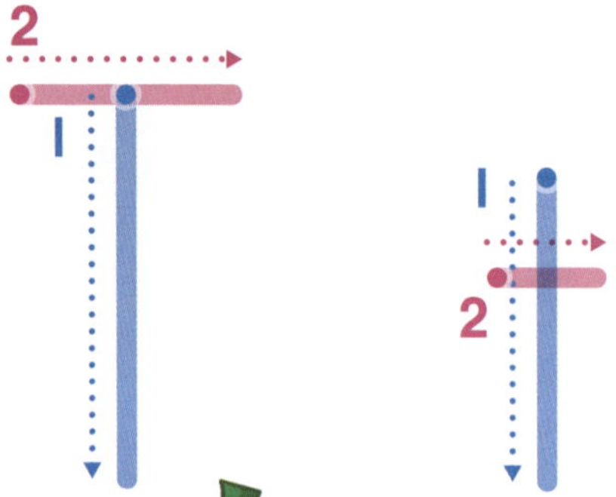

6 Trace, write, and say.

T

t

Vocabulary: **sun, soap, seed, table, tomato, tiger**

1 1.25 Listen and point. 2 Listen and repeat. Trace.

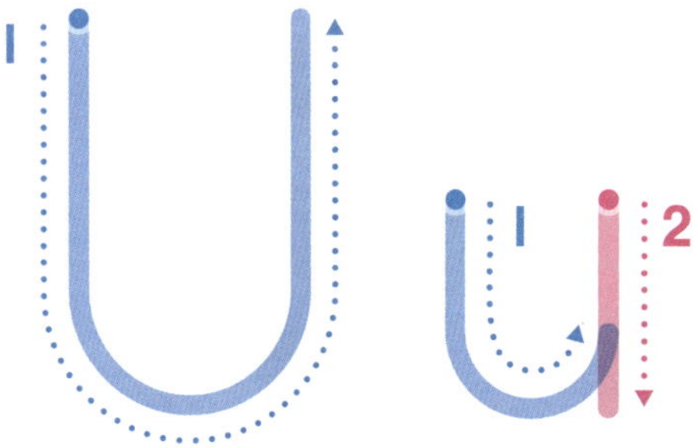

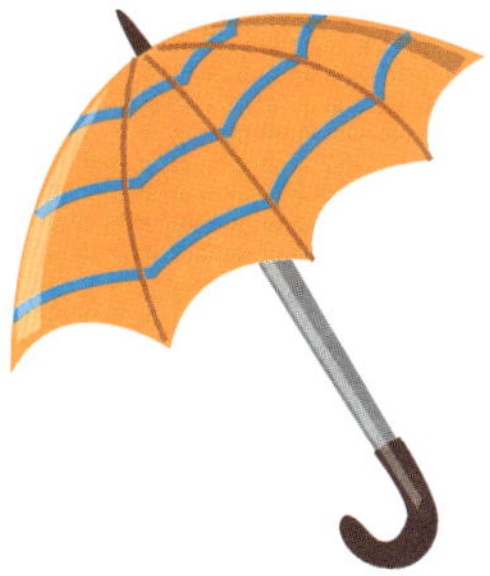

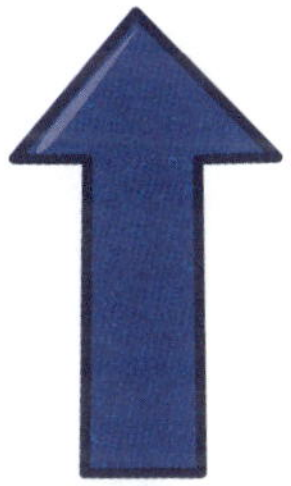

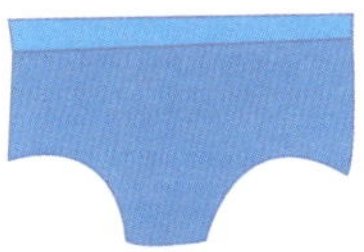

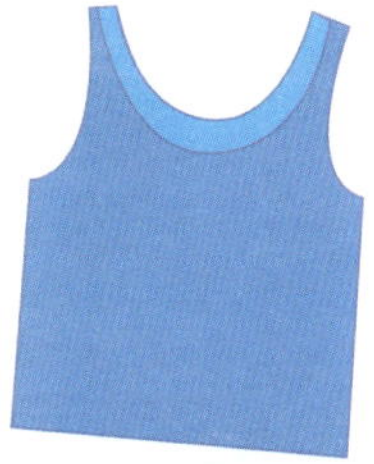

3 Trace, write, and say.

U

u

4 1.26 Listen, read, and match.

1 nut

2 bus

3 ten

4 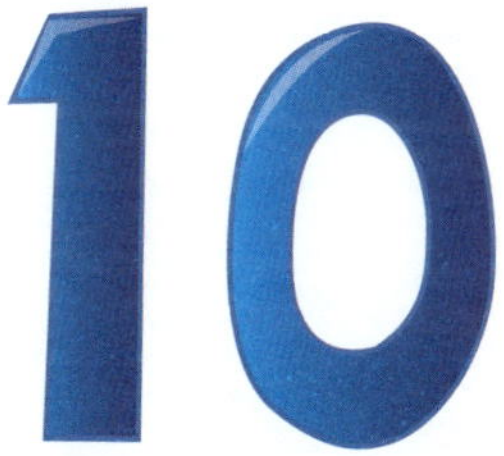 sad

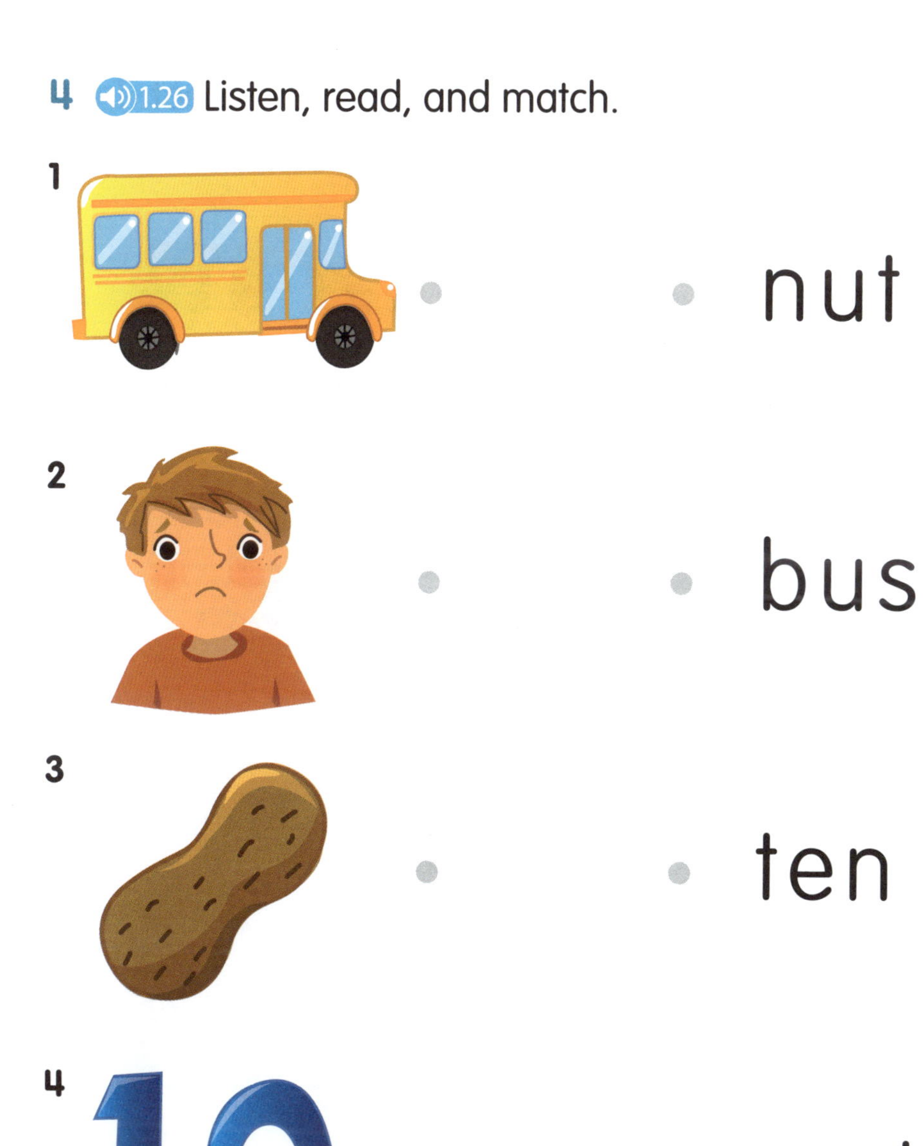

1 1.27 Listen and point. 2 Listen and repeat. Trace.

4 1.28 Listen and point. 5 Listen and repeat. Trace.

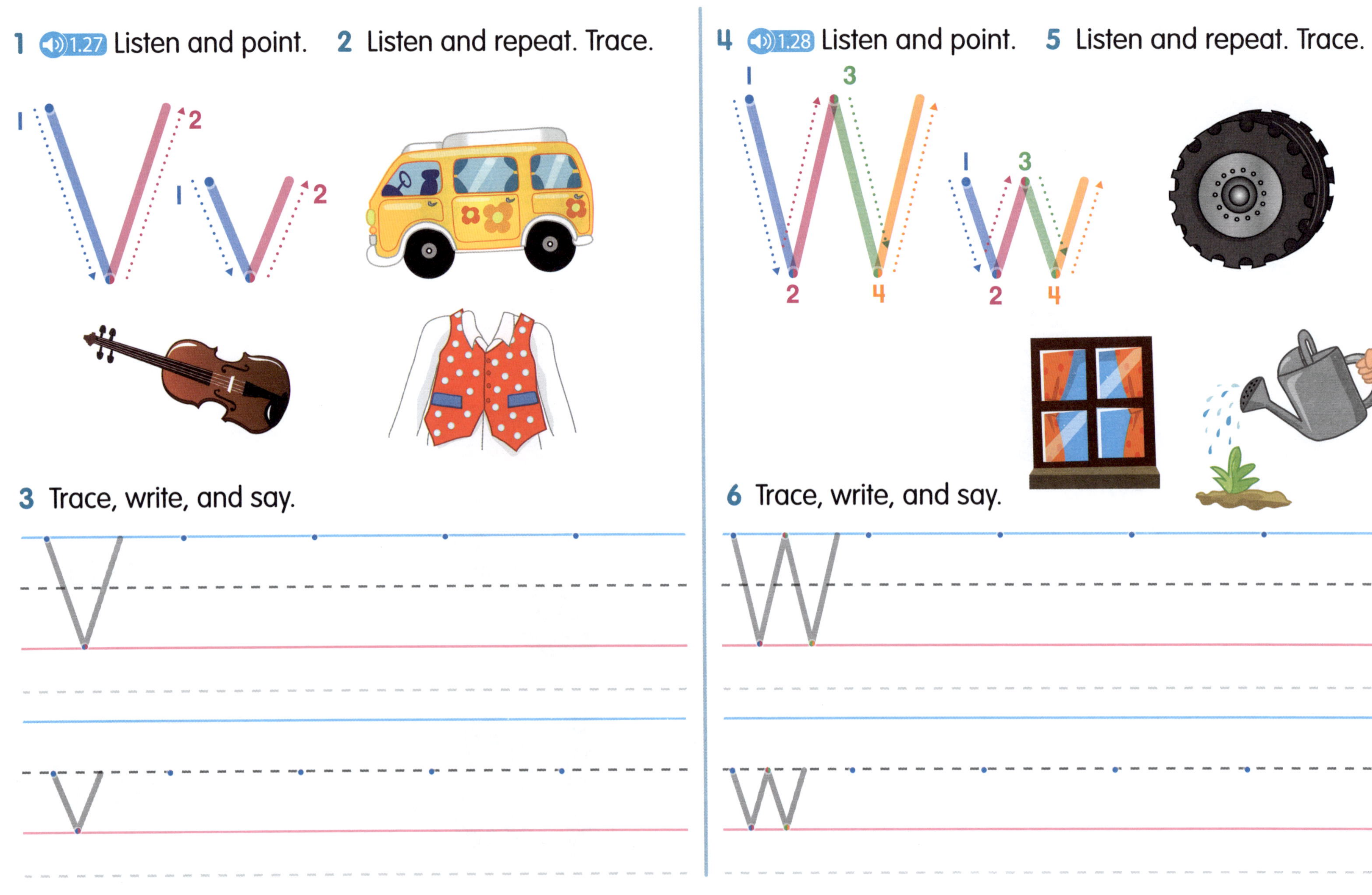

3 Trace, write, and say.

6 Trace, write, and say.

Vocabulary: van, violin, vest, wheel, window, water

1 1.29 Listen and point. 2 Listen and repeat. Trace.

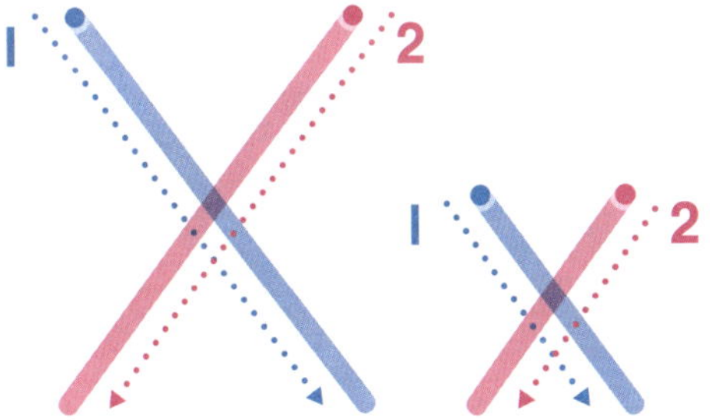

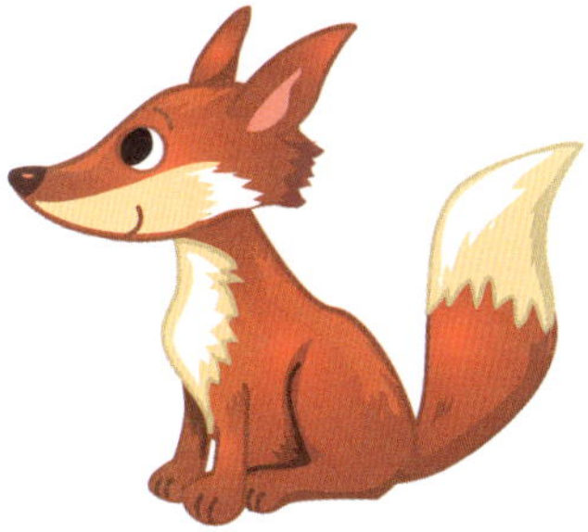

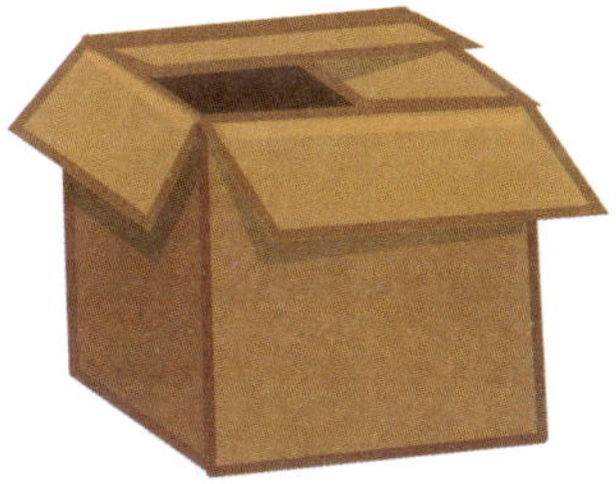

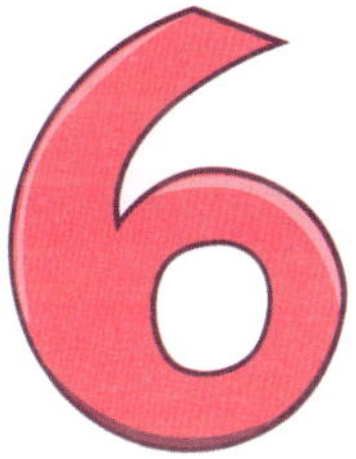

X x

3 Trace, write, and say.

X

x

4 1.30 Listen, read, and circle.

1 1.31 Listen and point. 2 Listen and repeat. Trace.

4 1.32 Listen and point. 5 Listen and repeat. Trace.

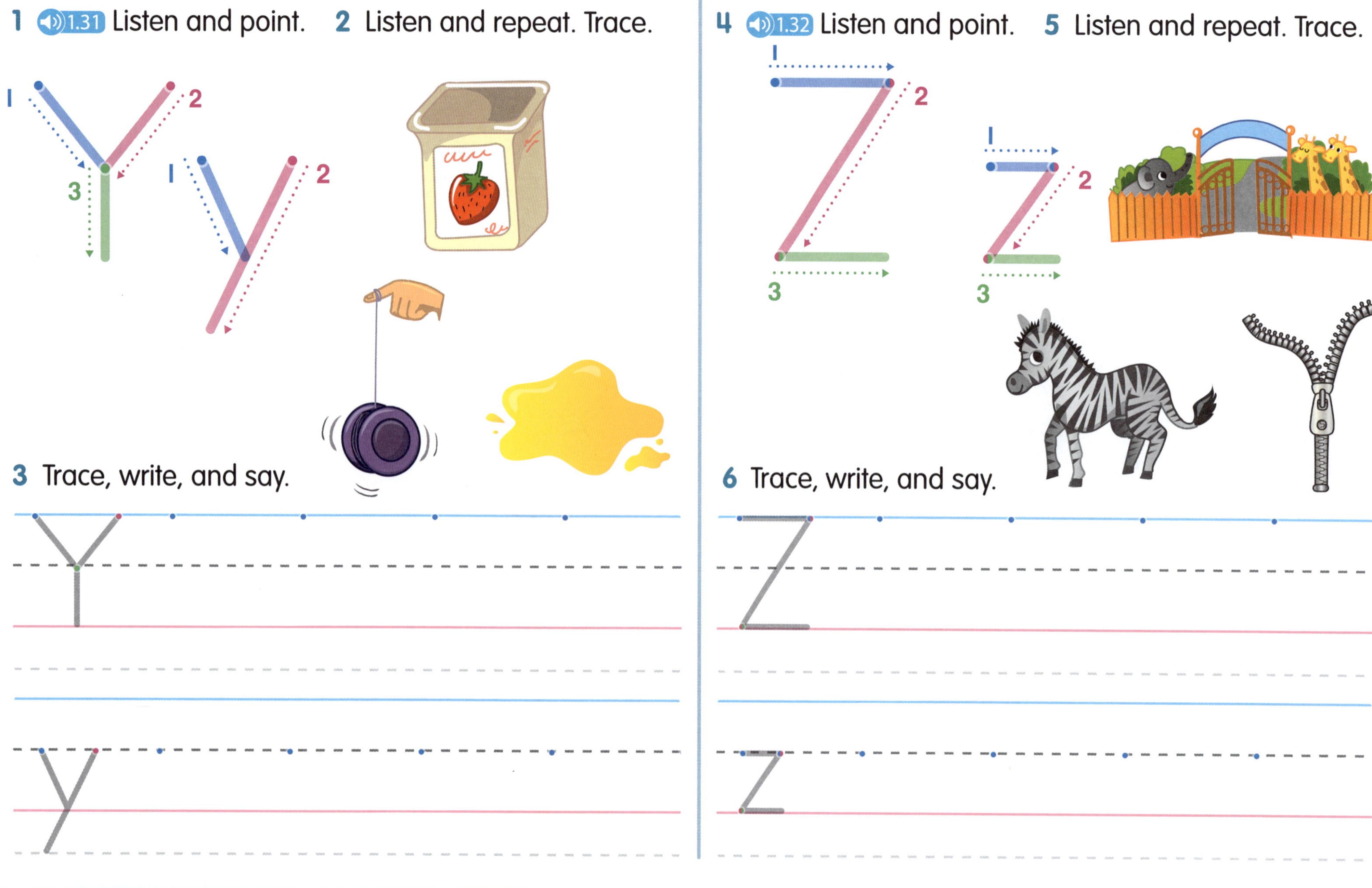

3 Trace, write, and say.

6 Trace, write, and say.

Hello
Alphabet letters and sounds: y, z

Vocabulary: yogurt, yo-yo, yellow, zoo, zebra, zipper

1 Read and match the rhyming words. 2 1.33 Listen and check.

six dog cat pen jug fan

hen van mix rug log bat

1 1.34 Listen and point. Listen and repeat.

Vocabulary: cat, cup, kite, key, **sock**, **neck**

1 1.35 Listen. Check (✓) the words with the **ck** sound at the end.

1

2

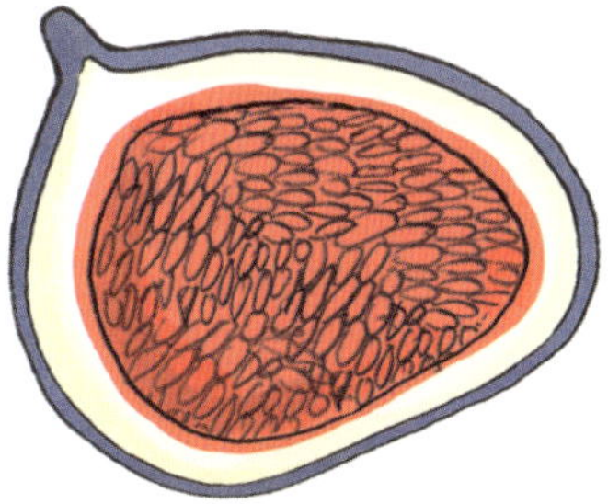

3

4

5

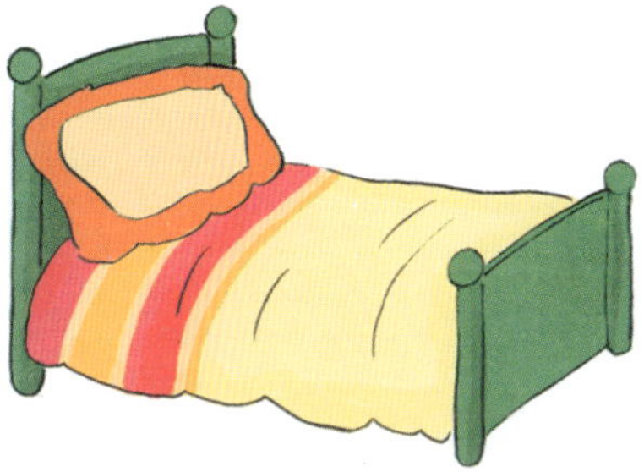

6

Vocabulary: **rock, fig, back, rat,** bed, cat

1 1.36 Listen and point. Listen and repeat.

1

cot

2

kid

3

duck

4

kick

1 1.37 Listen and match. Listen and repeat. **2** Read aloud.

It's a duck.

It's a red sock.

The cat is on the cot.

The kid can kick.

1 1.38 Listen and point. Listen and repeat.

sw

st

sk

sp

Vocabulary: swim, swing, stop, star, skip, skunk, spin, spider

1 1.39 Listen and circle the picture. **2** Trace.

1

sw sk

2

sp st

3

st sk

4

sp sw

1 Trace and say. **2** Match.

stack	skip	swim	spin

Vocabulary: spin, swim, **stack**, skip

1 1.40 Listen and follow. Listen and repeat. **2** Read aloud.

Pip can skip,
Jack can stack.
Lin can spin
On her back.
What can you do?

Sight words: can, on, **her, what, you, do**

1 1.41 Listen and point. Listen and repeat.

tr

fr

dr

cr

Vocabulary: truck, train, frog, friends, drum, dress, crab, crayon

1 1.42 Listen and match. 2 Trace.

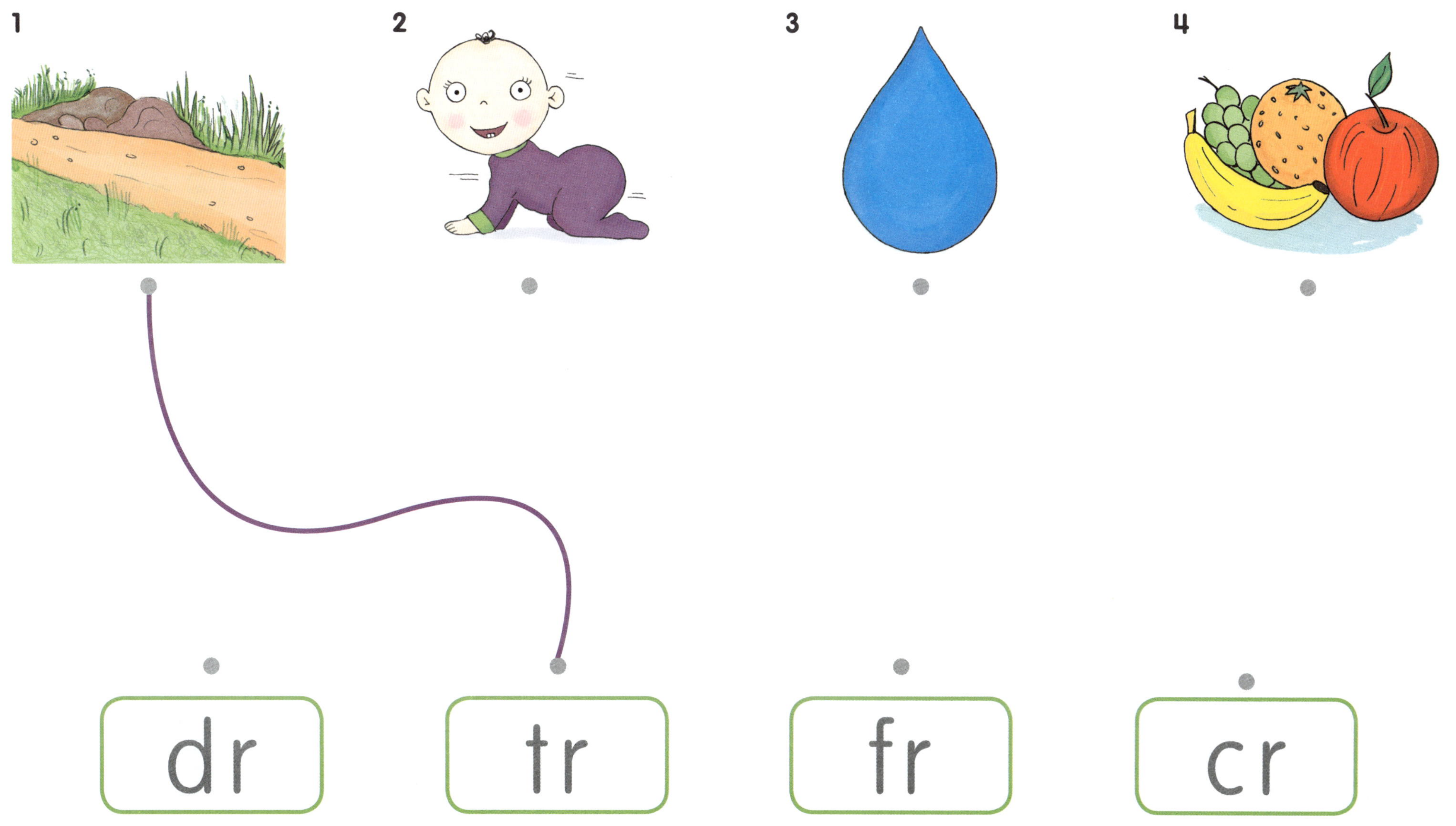

Vocabulary: track, crawl, drop, fruit

1 Trace and say. **2** Circle.

Vocabulary: crab, frog, track, dress, crayon, apple, truck, drop

1 1.43 Listen and chant.

Drip, drop, drip, drop,
In the pond, frogs hop.
Drop, drip, drop, drip,
On the track, I skip.

Sight words: in, the, on, I

1 1.44 Listen and point. Listen and repeat.

sl

bl

fl

cl

Vocabulary: sled, slide, black, blue, flower, sunflower, clock, cloud

1 1.45 Listen and circle. 2 Trace.

1

cl sl

2

fl bl

3

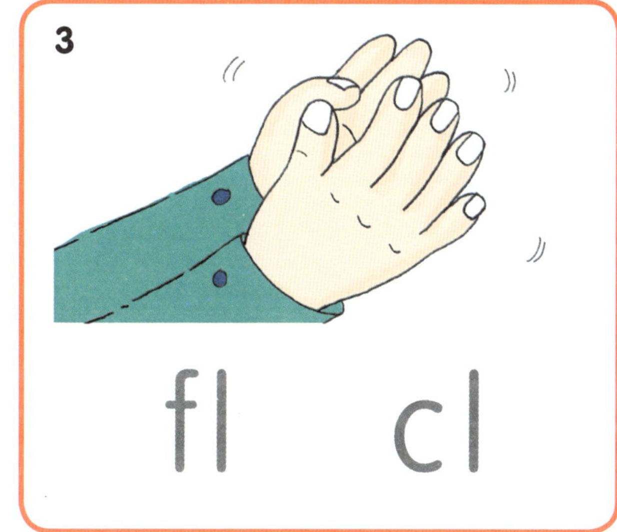

fl cl

4

sl cl

5

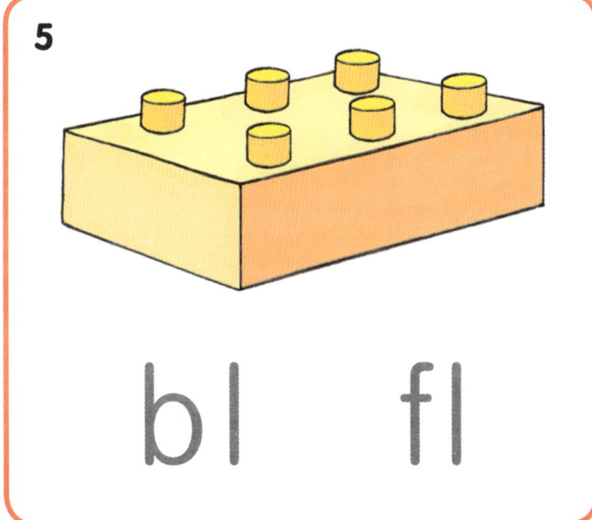

bl fl

6

cl fl

Vocabulary: slug, flap, clap, slip, block, fly

1 Trace and say. **2** Draw.

1 flag

2 sled

3 black

4 clock

Vocabulary: **flag,** sled, black, clock

1 1.46 Listen and match. Listen and repeat. 2 Read aloud.

The red hen clucks.

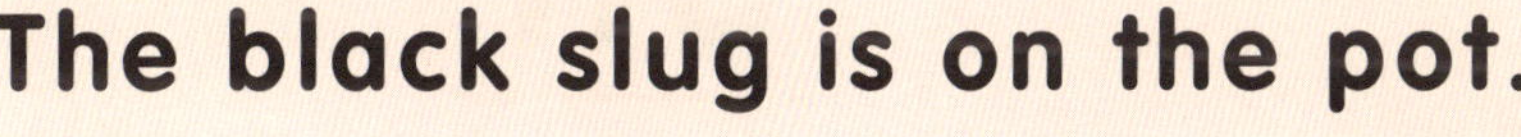

The black slug is on the pot.

The flag flaps in the wind.

The clock tick-tocks.

Sight words: the, is, on, in

1 1.47 Listen and point. Listen and repeat.

Vocabulary: shark, sheep, shoe, starfish, trash, brush

1 1.48 Listen and circle the sound you hear. Trace.

1

2 s sh

3 s sh

4 s sh

2 1.49 Write the letters. Listen and repeat.

1 Match and write. 2 Say.

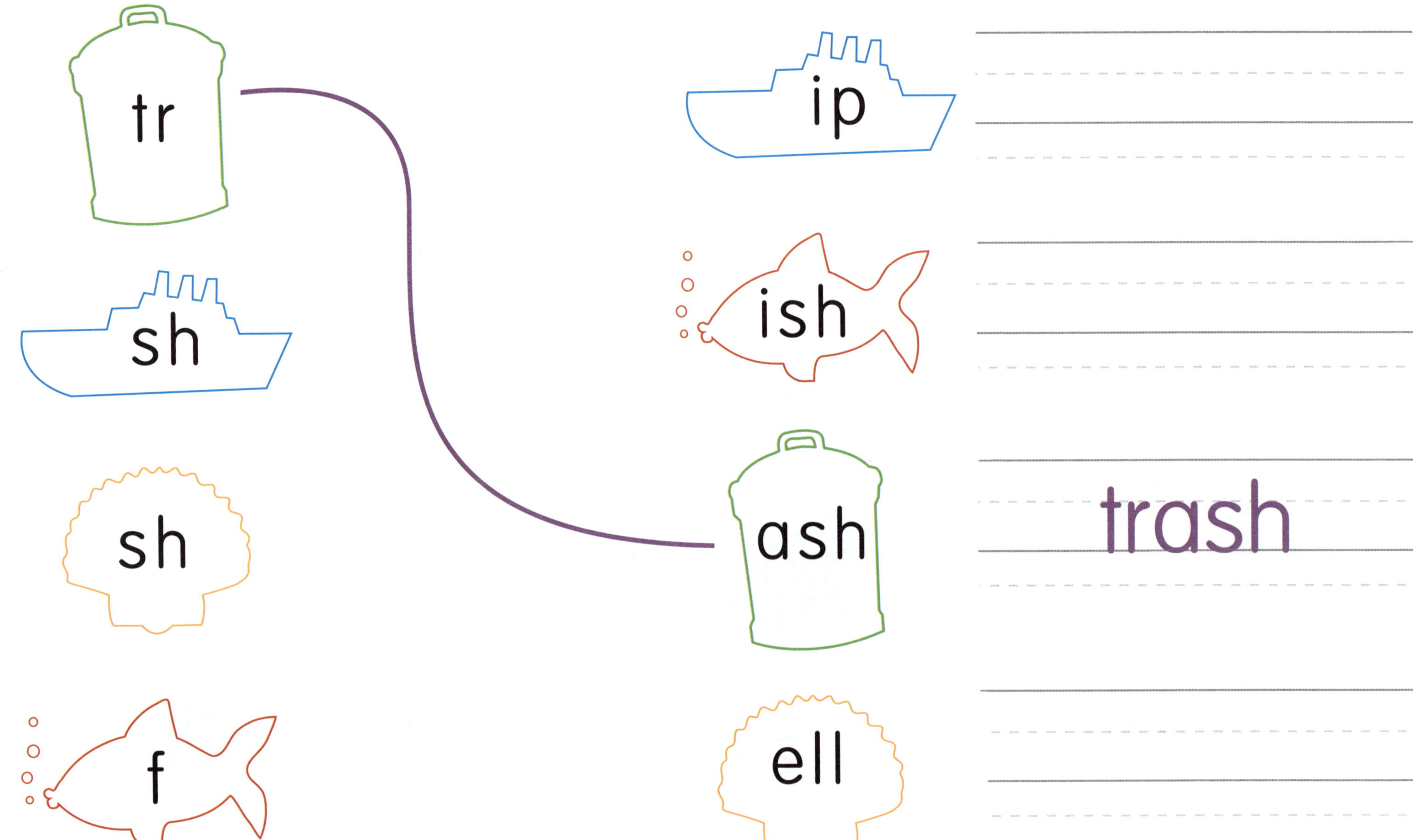

Vocabulary: trash, **ship**, **shell**, fish

1 1.50 Listen and follow. Listen and repeat. 2 Read aloud.

My Dish

1

My name is Ash.

2

This is my dish on the shelf.

3

Smash! Crash!

4

Careful, Ash!

Sight words: is, **this**, **my**, on, the

Unit 6

1 1.51 Listen and point. Listen and repeat.

Vocabulary: **chair, cheese, children, branch,** ostrich

1 1.52 Listen and circle the sound you hear. Trace.

1 ch sh

2 ch sh

3 ch sh

4 ch sh

2 1.53 Write the letters. Listen and repeat.

chin

ell

est

ben

1 Follow and write. 2 Say.

Vocabulary: bench, **chick**, **check**, **lunch**

1 1.54 Listen and follow. Listen and repeat. 2 Read aloud.

The Robin

1

The robin has a red chest.

2

She has six chicks in her nest.

3

The chicks have bugs for lunch.

4

The chicks get big!

Sight words: the, **has**, a, **she**, in, **her**, **have**, **for**

1 1.55 Listen and point. Listen and repeat.

Vocabulary: thorn, think, three, teeth, moth, bath

1 1.56 Listen and circle the sound you hear. Trace.

1 th s

2 th s

3 th s

4 th s

2 1.57 Write the letters. Listen and repeat.

math

ick

ink

clo

1 Match and write. 2 Say.

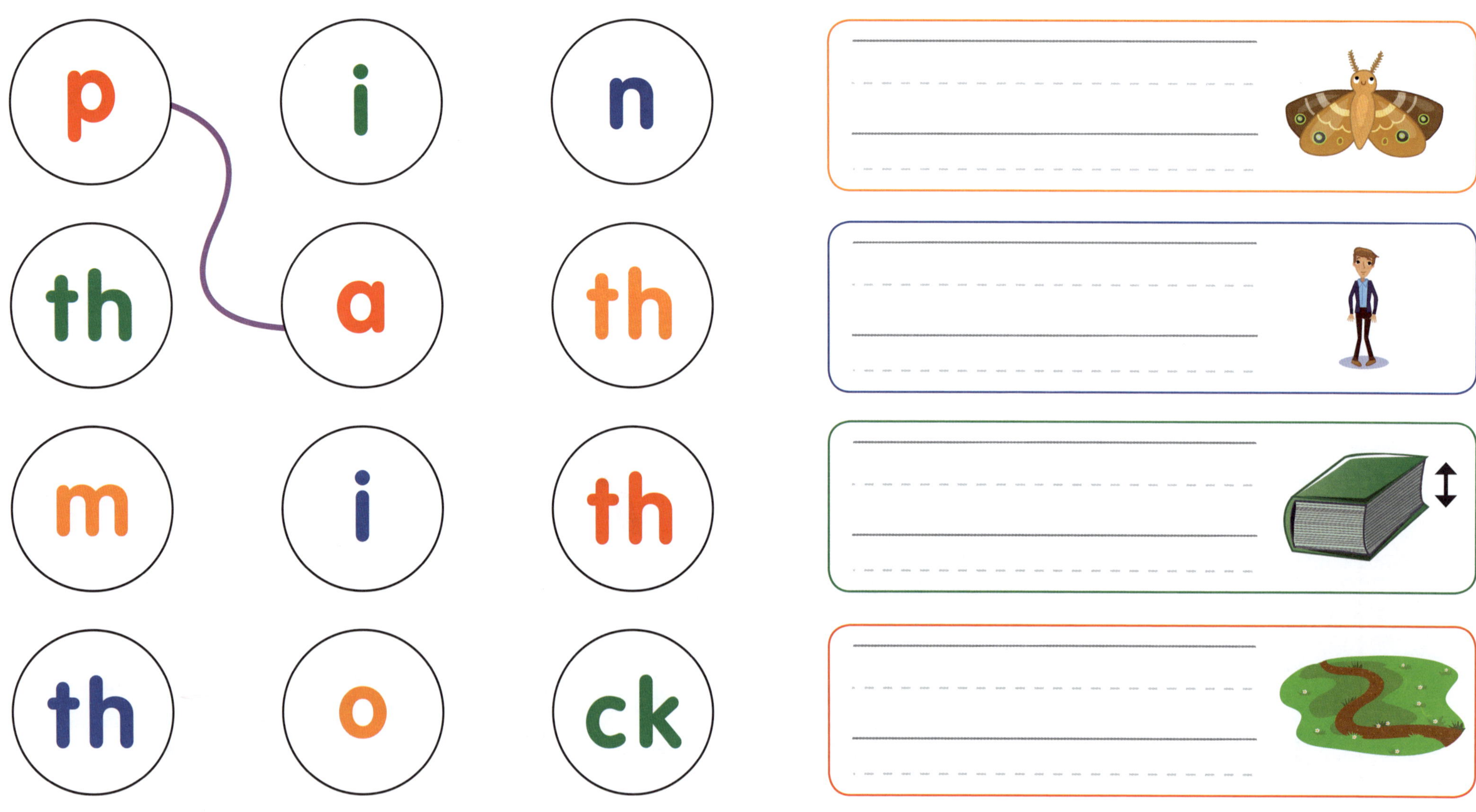

 Vocabulary: moth, **thin**, **thick**, **path**

1 1.58 Listen and match. Listen and repeat. 2 Read aloud.

A moth on the shelf,
A moth on the [chair],
A moth in the bath,
A moth in my [hair]!

A moth on the cloth,
A moth on the sink,
1, 2, 3, 4, 5,
6 moths, I think!

Sight words: a, the, on, in, my, I

1 1.59 Listen and point. Listen and repeat.

Vocabulary: clothes, that, this, feather, father, mother

1 1.60 Listen and circle the sound you hear. Trace.

1 th d

2 th d

3 th d

4 th d

2 1.61 Write the letters. Listen and repeat.

that

is

en

wi

Vocabulary: that, this, den, with

1 1.62 Listen and read. 2 Say.

The thin man with the hat thinks that the sun is hot.

3 Write the words in the correct circle.

~~the~~ ~~thin~~ with thinks that

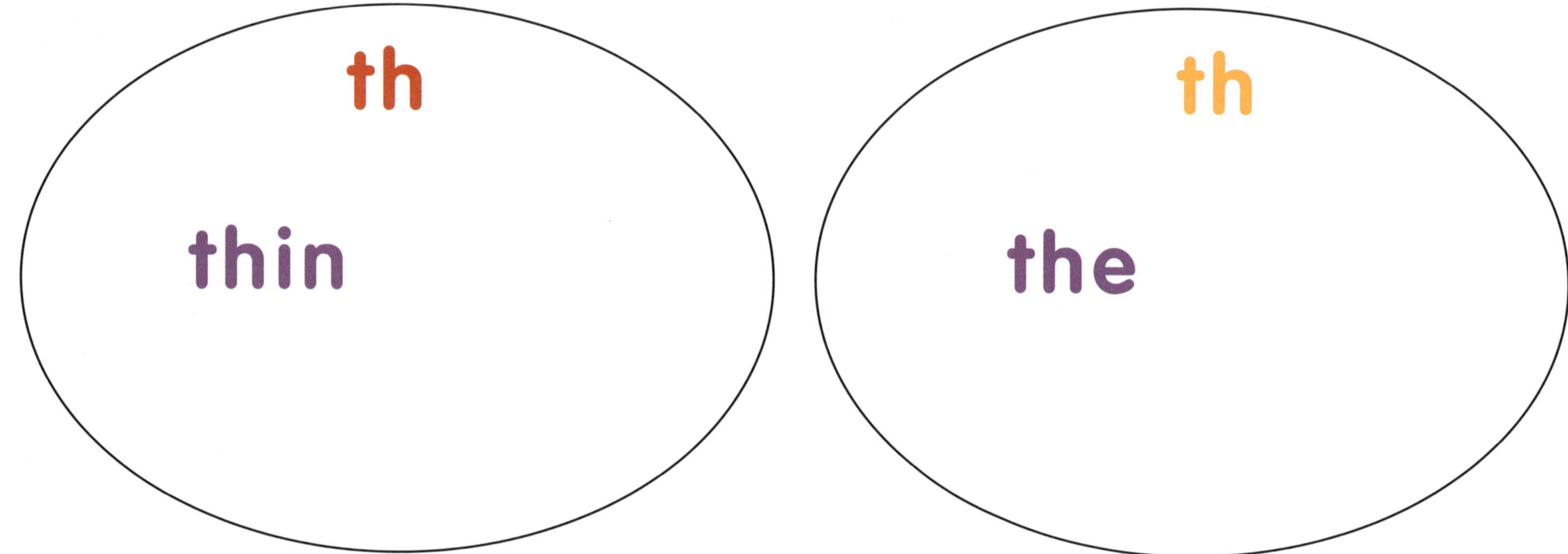

1 1.63 Listen and follow. Listen and repeat. 2 Read aloud.

Wet Clothes

1

This is Heather.
These are her brothers.

2

They are big. The weather is wet.
Splash!

3

Heather is sad.
Her clothes are wet.

4

She gets the bus.
Her brothers get wet!

Sight words: is, these, **are**, her, **they**, the, weather, she

1 1.64 Listen and point. Listen and repeat.

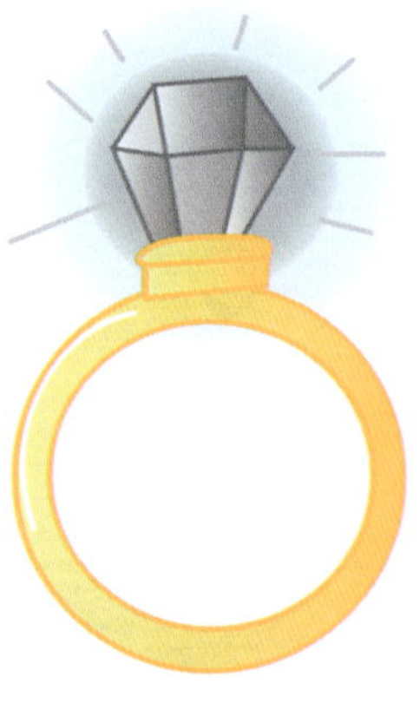

Vocabulary: ring, gong, bang, strong, king, hang

1 1.65 Listen and circle the sound you hear. Trace.

1 n ng

2 n ng

3 n ng

4 n ng

2 1.66 Write the letters. Listen and repeat.

sing

ru

lo

wi

Vocabulary: sing, run, long, wing

1 Match and write. **2** Say.

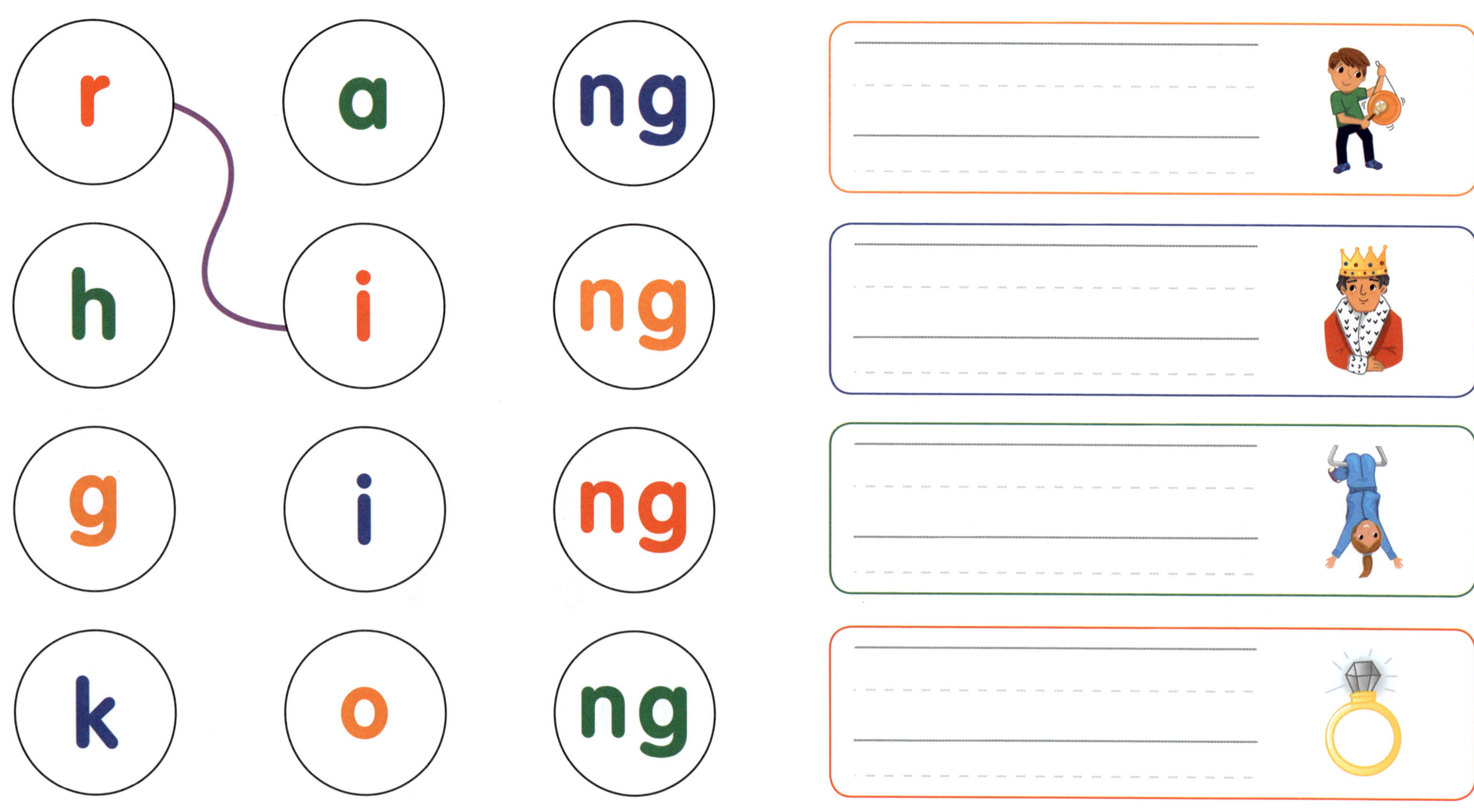

Vocabulary: gong, king, hang, ring

1 1.67 Listen and chant.

Sing it, sing it, sing it with me.
Sing it, yes, sing along.

I hop and I skip,
I run on the track,
I kick a ⚽,
I swim on my back,
I bang on a drum,
It's lots of fun.
But the best thing is a song!

Sight words: **it, me, yes, I, and,** on, the, a, my, **of,** is

Great Clarendon Street, Oxford, OX2 6DP, United Kingdom

Oxford University Press is a department of the University of Oxford. It furthers the University's objective of excellence in research, scholarship, and education by publishing worldwide. Oxford is a registered trade mark of Oxford University Press in the UK and in certain other countries

First published in 2018
2024
10 9

ISBN: 978 0 19 405480 5

Printed in China

This book is printed on paper from certified and well-managed sources

ACKNOWLEDGEMENTS

Back cover photograph: Oxford University Press building/David Fisher

Cover artwork by: Rob McClurkan/Bright Agency and Mike Garton/Bright Agency (in the style of Rob McClurkan)

Illustrations by: Kirsten Collier/Bright Agency pp.21, 23, 27, 31, 33, 37, 39, 41, 43, 45, 47, 49, 51, 55; Amanda Enright/Advocate-Art pp.2, 3, 4, 5, 6, 7, 8, 9, 10, 11, 12, 13, 14, 15, 16, 17, 18, 19, 20, 22, 24, 25, 26, 28, 29, 30, 32, 34, 35, 36, 38, 40, 42, 44, 46, 48, 50, 52, 53, 54.